THE
AIKIDO
STUDENT
HANDBOOK

GREG O'CONNOR

BLUE SNAKE BOOKS
Berkeley, California

Published by Blue Snake Books/Frog, Ltd.

Blue Snake Books/Frog, Ltd. books are distributed by
North Atlantic Books
P.O. Box 12327
Berkeley, California 94712

Cover design, layout, graphics, illustrations, and cartoons by
    Greg O'Connor
Production by Hal Meyers and Paula Morrison
Printed in the United States of America
Distributed to the book trade by Publishers Group West

PLEASE NOTE: The creators and publishers of this book disclaim any liabilities for loss in connection with following any of the practices, exercises, and advice contained herein. To reduce the chance of injury or any other harm, the reader should consult a professional before undertaking this or any other martial arts, movement, meditative arts, health, or exercise program. The instructions and advice printed in this book are in not any way intended as a substitute for medical, mental, or emotional counseling with a licensed physician or healthcare provider.

Library of Congress-Cataloging-in-Publication Data

O'Connor, Greg, 1954–
    The Aikido Student Handbook / Greg O'Connor
        p.   cm.
    Includes index.
    ISBN 1-883319-04-8
    1. Aikido I. Title.
    GV1114.35.O34   1993
    796.8'154 — dc20   93-25763
                                                          CIP

THE
AIKIDO
STUDENT
HANDBOOK

This *Aikido Student Handbook* is dedicated to the Founder of
Aikido, Morihei Ueshiba (1883–1969). May it help in some
small way to bring about the peace he envisioned.

And to the memory and spirit of Terry Dobson (1937–1992),
friend and mentor, whom I will miss terribly.

Acknowledgments

I want to thank Sensei Rick Stickles for introducing me to Aikido and for all his help, guidance and friendship throughout the years. As a student in his dojo he encouraged me to seek out and train with as many teachers as possible and to be open to what they had to offer. Because of this encouragement and his life's choices, I am teaching Aikido today. For this and many other things I will always be truly thankful.

I also gratefully acknowledge and thank Yoshimitsu Yamada Sensei for all his years of generosity, understanding, and support. His ongoing work to bring people together both here in the United States and the world over is an inspiration. He truly is "Mr. Nice Guy!"

Special thanks to Hal Meyers for all his help and enthusiasm and for the "magic" he performed on his Mac in putting this handbook together. Without his generosity, this project would not have been possible.

Special thanks, also, to Terry Dobson for his wonderful encouragement and endorsement of this finished project just two weeks before he left us forever.

Also, my appreciation goes to Bruce Bookman (5th Dan, Chief Instructor Seattle Aikikai) for his valuable commentary on initial first drafts of this work.

As always, many "behind the scenes" people contributed their advice, suggestions, and professional expertise to this project. My sincere gratitude to them all.

I want to thank, also, everyone who has ever helped me on my personal Aikido path. That includes all the gifted teachers with whom I've had the honor of training, all of my practice partners, both agreeable and not, and the guy who cut me off this morning on the freeway.

Table of Contents

Preface 9

Foreword 10

Introduction. 13

About the Founder 15

About Aikido 17

What You Will Get from Aikido. 19

The True Power of Aikido 21

What is a Dojo? 24

Looking for a Dojo 28

Common Questions 30

Joining a Dojo 35

Etiquette. 47

Training in Aikido. 53

Weapons Training—Boken and Jo 73

Promotion and Advancement 76

Conclusion 79

U.S.A.F. Test Requirements 82

Aikido Terms 86

Suggested Reading 102

Preface

MY PURPOSE IN creating this *Aikido Student Handbook* is to answer questions—sometimes voiced, sometimes not—by the first day- or the *ten thousandth-*day student. I'll try to explain those things you would like to ask, forgot to ask, or were never told.

This book will guide you through the Aikido dojo, Aikido etiquette, and give you advice on Aikido training. It will tell you what to expect, what is expected of you as a student in Aikido, and much more.

In the following pages I offer personal observations and findings accumulated from my own Aikido training. Keep in mind that this is not a book on technique, but rather an introduction to the spirit of Aikido training. I hope it provides you with some thought and guidance as you refer to it from time to time throughout your study of Aikido.

The World (as well as the world of Aikido) has many languages and environments. Your mission, should you choose to accept it, is to learn about yourself and to better your character and the way it honors, accepts, adapts, and grows within whatever environment you happen to be at any given moment.

"Remember, wherever you go—there you are."
— *Buckaroo Banzai*

The trick is to be at peace—wherever you are.

Greg O'Connor

Foreword

I WOULD LIKE TO congratulate Greg on the completion of *The Aikido Student Handbook*. The project has been no small task. A great deal of time and thought was put into what I feel is one of the most comprehensive works of this kind.

Aikido is a process. A martial process, yes, but more importantly, a process by which we attempt to bring about a balance between our physical, mental, and spiritual selves. Not unlike other mind/body/spirit integration disciplines, Aikido is merely one path an individual may choose to improve the quality of life and come to a basic understanding of the nature of being human.

Martial arts, yoga, meditation, movement, and bodyworking therapies are some of the techniques we use to bring us to a singular destination. To describe or "label" this destination is a difficult task. Some believe it to be a state of personal clarity that enables us to connect in a healthy way with others and the environment which surrounds us all. It is through this type of connection that we may have a positive effect on the world around us.

You may choose Aikido as a possible road to achieve this type of balance. On the following pages, Greg will give you some useful tools to help accomplish the task.

This book, however, is much more than a simple "how to" guide about the practice of Aikido. It is an example of the author's commitment to the "Do," or the path of personal growth. It reflects the clarity we seek in an attempt to actually make a difference. It's intention is to help guide the student on a journey of the greatest magnitude—the examination of the techniques and principles of Aikido and of O Sensei's message to the world. Use it wisely.

Rick Stickles
5th Dan, Shidoin
Chief Instructor
ASNJ-Elizabeth
ASNJ-Red Bank

Yoshimitsu Yamada
8th Dan, Shihan
Direct Student of the Founder
Chairman of the U.S.A.F.
Chief Instructor New York Aikikai

Introduction

I N THE PAST twenty years or so, the Aikido population has increased tremendously in the United States. Among the many reasons for this, one notable fact is that American instructors are doing a good job!

Needless to say, the purpose of studying Aikido is not only to gain physical ability. We practice for the deeper reason to become better human beings. For that reason I highly recommend this *Aikido Student Handbook* by Mr. Greg O'Connor. I believe this book will be beneficial not only for those who are just starting Aikido, but for those already involved and particularly for those who hold teaching positions.

It is my sincere wish that there will be more American students becoming Aikido instructors and that they realize that the responsibility of a teacher is not just teaching what they already know but continuing to practice and learn more about Aikido themselves, so that they constantly become better teachers for the benefit of everybody.

Congratulations Mr. O'Connor, for your excellent *Aikido Student Handbook*.

Yoshimitsu Yamada

"Aikido is the principle of nonresistance."

—*Morihei Ueshiba*
The Founder of Aikido

About the Founder

THE FOUNDER OF Aikido was someone who, probably like yourself, sought to be at peace no matter what the circumstances. He wished to maintain a harmonious connection with all things at all times. As years passed and his martial abilities became quite phenomenal, he spoke more and more about our global human family and the necessity for each person to be open to the ways of nature and the universe; to have a love and respect for all beings with the goal to heal ourselves and the world.

The product of his life and his gift to you is Aikido.

He was born Morihei Ueshiba in 1883 in the Japanese fishing and farming village of Tanabe. His name, Morihei, meaning "abundant peace," was prophetic.

He began his study of the martial arts in his youth. He trained first in sumo, then traditional sword, spear, and ju jitsu, while at the same time feeding a voracious appetite for mathematics, physics, and spiritual studies. Investing years in training, his prowess and reputation as a renowned master of the martial arts grew. His reputation attracted many challengers who came to test their skills and refute the increasingly legendary Ueshiba. He would inevitably defeat them all—many even asked to become his students. After one such encounter in which he easily evaded an attacker's repeated strikes with a wooden sword, doing so without injuring his challenger, he had an enlightening revelation. Winning as a result of defeating another was not truly winning at all. From that point on his deep spiritual beliefs and his remarkable martial art became one.

In 1941, O Sensei (Great Teacher), as he later came to be known, began calling his martial system Aikido, "the way of harmony and love." He still attracted many people, but this time they came in wonder and awe of a living legend and the power of his Aikido.

O Sensei maintained a simple lifestyle all his life and kept a strong attachment to the earth through his farming. He loved every aspect of it: working the soil, planting, nurturing, and harvesting. He did the same with his Aikido. It has now grown all over the world— millions of seedlings growing and spreading the nourishment of Aikido.

O Sensei saw the great potential of Aikido to create global healing and encouraged his students to give it to the world. The purpose of Aikido, he maintained, "is to build a heaven on earth by bringing people together in friendship and harmony. I teach this art to help my students learn how to serve their fellow beings."

O Sensei died on April 26, 1969, but not before visiting the United States and seeing his beloved Aikido being taught and practiced not only in Japan but all around the world.

About Aikido

"Aikido is the spirit of loving protection for all beings."
—*Morihei Ueshiba*

M AKE NO MISTAKE about it. Aikido is a devastating martial art, the full power of which is rarely seen. Those who do not realize this simply do not know Aikido. An Aikidoist who knows this power will only demonstrate their full abilities on another Aikidoist who is fully trained to receive and survive it.

When people first observe Aikido they see the spectacular throws. They see the attackers fall and roll, but are often skeptical as to the real effectiveness of Aikido technique until they have actually felt and received an Aikido technique. They then realize that the "cooperation" with which they saw the attackers falling—"like it was rehearsed"—is absolutely necessary to avoid serious injury. Those attackers are also demonstrating their knowledge of Aikido by blending with a powerful technique and showing how they can survive it safely.

The first time you feel an Aikido technique such as *kotegaeshi* or *nikkyo,* you are shocked and surprised by its power and simple effectiveness. You learn immediately that it is wise not to resist, but to respect it and move your body accordingly so as to avoid injury.

All movement in Aikido is circular. Even if it appears direct and linear there are subtle spiral motions involved. Aikido techniques are designed to follow the body's natural movement. Joints are turned and exaggerated along their natural

17

range of motion. This motivates the attacker to fall without damaging the joint. Aikido pins are designed with the same idea in mind and can be applied to and by anyone of any size with little or no effort.

Aikido principles hold to a defensive mode rather than to an offensive one. One tends to lose his or her balance and inner peace when aggression is allowed to run the mind. The Aikidoist learns to trust natural instincts and intuition and to act appropriately without sacrificing internal equilibrium.

This does not mean that we should lay down and passively accept everything that comes our way; rather, we should respect it, keep a good heart, and redirect it with a strong flow of life-affirming energy.

This applies to life on and off the mat. You do not have to be strong, big, fast, or, for that matter, athletic, to learn and become accomplished at Aikido. A simple desire for peace is all that is needed. Use your intuition. When you sense a threat, recognize it, accept it, and respect its nature and intention. Allow it to blend with your nature, then maintain your balance and control and redirect it safely.

It can be said that Aikido is a martial art for people who desire true peace—the peace that comes from "the loving protection of all beings."

What You Will Get from Aikido

"Through Aikido, extend all your powers to achieve peaceful harmony with the world."
—Morihei Ueshiba

THE TIME YOU spend in Aikido will be quality time. It will enrich you significantly with benefits literally too numerous to describe in these pages—but that will not stop me from trying.

You will discover that while practicing Aikido's sophisticated techniques you will be enriching your whole being. A holistically healthy physical, mental, emotional, and spiritual state results from Aikido's multi-level experience. Both hemispheres of the brain, for example, learn to work together incorporating the intuition and feelings of the right brain with the analytical abilities of the left. People who are predominantly "right brain" or "left brain" find themselves becoming much more integrated. The increased self-confidence and awareness you will attain will enable a real feeling of balance and control to emerge in your life.

In recent years the powerful positive effect of Aikido has been recognized by many major corporations and learning institutions. Aikido principles are now being taught by highly respected organizations as ideal methods for handling conflict resolution and stress reduction.

You, too, will find that one of the best remedies for stress is a visit to the dojo. The benefits you will get from an hour of Aikido will go a lot farther than time spent worrying, visiting the local "watering hole," or an evening spent blankly in front of the TV. What's more, you will most likely have, upon leaving the dojo, not only a fresh outlook, but an *increase* in energy. (Don't ask me to explain it—endorphins, perhaps!—but it happens.)

Your body, as well as your mind and character, will inevitably change, gaining strength, flexibility, and resilience. Increased cardiovascular fitness, respiration, and overall muscle tone will allow for a natural flow of energy. You will find that Aikido training develops not only a strong, supple body but a strong, supple character as well, able to stand with great dignity yet adjust to all of life's challenges. Aikido is, to borrow a phrase from Rudyard Kipling, a way to "keep your head when all around you are losing theirs." Sound good? In Aikido you learn just that—how to keep your balance in the midst of adversity. A balance that is maintained physically, mentally, emotionally, and spiritually.

Another advantage of the dojo are your new friends and fellow students who provide a high-quality support system with similar goals and challenges as yourself. It seems (and I may be a bit biased in this opinion) that Aikido attracts the best of people. They are easygoing, sincere, and have a healthy blend of maturity and humor, coming together in an atmosphere of cooperation and camaraderie. A strong sense of healthy community is felt, and that feeling is incorporated into our lives outside the dojo.

The True Power of Aikido

*"I want considerate people to listen to the voice of Aikido.
It is not for correcting others; it is for correcting your own
mind. This is Aikido. This is the mission of Aikido and
should be your mission."*
—Morihei Ueshiba

A IKIDO IS A martial art. You will find out on the mat, and
later in your own life, just how powerful it is. The more
you practice it, the more you will acquire that power.
Remember, however, that as your technical abilities increase,
the greater your capacity for compassion, restraint, and patience must be. Protecting your attacker along with yourself
is the purpose and beauty of Aikido. Simply defeating someone else is not. Remind yourself each time you step on the
mat of this "prime directive."

In Aikido, a unique approach is exercised to handle an attack. Rather than clashing with or blocking the attack, Aikido's circular flowing techniques blend with it. The attack is
welcomed, enveloped, absorbed, and then redirected by the
mind and actions of the Aikidoist. The throws and pins of
Aikido are extremely powerful and effective. Therefore, once
you are blending with an attack, great care should be taken
while completing the technique to keep in mind the welfare
of your practice partner. A safe conclusion should result for
both individuals.

The self-defense techniques of Aikido have quite a wide
range of application—from the gentlest to the most severe.
They can be devastating, ending an attack with sudden deci-

siveness, or dissipating it with the essence of a soft breeze. Having these options, we learn all the levels of applying a technique. Even in slow practice we can build power and intensity, yet keep it in check. This range allows you to exercise an ethical choice in resolving the interaction with your partner. This is a rare opportunity for personal growth that empowers those who recognize and take advantage of it.

"Competition" in Aikido

There is no "competition" in Aikido; at least not in the conventional sense. In traditional Aikido there are no contests, competitions, or tournaments. Real Aikido is not a sport.

Competition creates the dynamics of a win/lose scenario. Aikido, however, allows for a win/win resolution to any conflict—an outcome that results in mutual benefit and peace for all involved.

Competition is "survival of the fittest" and promotes the idea of the strong dominating the weak; victor and vanquished. With Aikido, however, the strong support, guide, and nurture the weak. Therefore, both actually become stronger in their body and their being.

The only competition you will find in Aikido is the most challenging type. You compete with the learned behavior within yourself that keeps you from being at peace and in harmony, and which keeps you from accepting, blending with, and executing a technique while caring for your partner. As you continue your Aikido practice, you will find that you can accomplish all these things by resolving your inner conflict.

"Destroy the foe that's hidden in the body."

— Morihei Ueshiba

"Noncompetition, in O Sensei's words, is training the self. In order for humans to achieve their highest potential, they must go through it. Competition as a basis for development leads to ego inflation. This is no way for a human to realize his potential. The value of what he or she is cannot be determined by other people. It is a lonely path. Don't compare with others. Even if no one knows, heaven and earth know, and those who know, know."

—Arikawa Sensei

What Is a Dojo?

A dojo can be defined as:
- *a place where the Way (in this case the way of Aikido) is practiced.*
- *a place for forging the body and the spirit.*
- *a place of enlightenment.*

A DOJO IS NOT a gym for mere "working out." It is more than just a building. It is a sacred place that cannot be defined by its geographical location, the height of its walls, or the value of its contents. It is defined by the spirit emanating from it and within it—individual, collective, and universal spirit. A dojo should be appreciated by seeing it with one's heart.

Entering the Dojo

Upon entering the dojo you remove your shoes. This symbolizes leaving behind your material day, your ego, and "your troubles at the door." This, of course, also helps keep the dojo clean, free of tracked-in soil and the like.

A typical dojo usually contains the following:

The Kamiza

As you look around, your eye will probably be drawn to a focal point at the head of the mat area. This area is known as the *kamiza* or *shomen*.

The kamiza is a shrine to the founder and to the spirit (kami) of Aikido. It usually contains a photo of the Founder and a brushed Japanese calligraphy for inspiration. Perhaps there will be a meditation bell or a sword. Sometimes a small, tastefully arranged display of flowers or a bonsai (dwarf tree) is included to give balance to the dojo and to the martial training spirit we cultivate there. When entering or leaving the dojo or stepping onto or off of the mat, all bows are directed towards the kamiza. Also, upon opening or closing class, the instructor and students bow together towards the kamiza.

The Mat

The mat area is where Aikido practice takes place. It should be kept clean. Shoes are *never* worn on the mat. Before stepping onto the mat, be sure that the bottoms of your feet as well as your hands, face, and *gi* (white traditional uniform), are absolutely clean (see Personal Hygiene, pg. 36).

Dressing Rooms

The dojo usually contains both men's and women's dressing rooms. They should be kept as clean and neat as the rest of the dojo. Upon leaving the dressing rooms, please clean up after yourself (and others if necessary) and make sure you are not leaving any of your belongings (jewelry, umbrellas, car keys, secret documents, underwear, etc.) behind for someone else to ponder and pick up.

Bulletin Boards

There may be bulletin boards located throughout the dojo. They provide important information and are constantly changing. Make it a habit, along with taking your shoes off and signing in, to always check them. Information about upcoming seminars at that dojo or other dojos is usually posted, as well as interesting tidbits of "aiki" news. If you offer a service and would like to display information or your business card, ask permission of the chief instructor first.

Weapons and Weapons Rack

The dojo may contain wall racks where *boken* (wooden swords) and *jo* (wooden staffs) are stored. They are the property of the dojo and are there for the convenience of the members. These weapons remain in the dojo at all times. If you have the privilege of using them, make sure you return them to their proper storage rack. Always inspect your weapons for cracks and splinters. If you find any damages, bring them to the instructor's attention.

Ranking Sticks

The small wooden sticks inscribed with names that you may see hanging on the wall of the dojo are ranking sticks. Anyone who has earned *kyu* rank and above is included there, as well as the instructors of the dojo.

Sign-in/Attendance Sheet

Each dojo usually contains a sign-in sheet that students log on for each class they attend. This is a record of the classes they have attended which is then verified prior to any promotional testing.

The Office

The dojo office is where the chief instructor conducts all dojo business. When approaching the office, be mindful of the activity that may already be in progress and wait your turn. If the instructor is busy, on the phone or with another student, he or she still wants to see you. Have patience for a moment while the instructor finishes the business at hand. When meeting with an instructor in the office (or office area), remember to be courteous, excuse yourself if you must interrupt, and thank him or her after you are finished.

The Phone

Always ask permission before using the dojo phone. Please keep all calls brief.

Looking for a Dojo

THE BEST WAY to learn about Aikido philosophy and techniques is on the mat in regular, trial-and-error training with a good instructor. To do so, don't merely look for a school, look for a teacher.

Research the instructors and the schools in your area. The dojo may be the teacher's basement or garage, a YMCA, or a ten thousand square foot traditional dojo. The surroundings do not matter nearly as much as the character of the teacher and the quality of the teaching.

Make an appointment to meet with and speak to the instructor. Ask him or her politely about their credentials. Where did they receive their training? Are they certified? How do you feel about him/her? What is the atmosphere in the dojo? How does it feel to you? Observe a few classes to get a feel for the

quality and style of training. (Be wary if instructors are reluctant to allow you to observe before signing up.) Methods, customs, styles and etiquette will vary from dojo to dojo. Take notice of the students practicing. What is their attitude? Are they enjoying themselves? Do they support and help one another? Are they concerned about each other's safety? Trust your gut feeling. If you feel right about the teacher and the dojo, join it.

Common Questions

Here are some answers to the questions most often asked after visiting some Aikido dojos:

Is Aikido effective as a martial art?
Yes, though you may need to practice diligently for some time to realize that for yourself.

Is Aikido considered a "soft" or "hard" style?
It is both. It can be extremely gentle and esoteric, or brutally decisive, capable of severely injuring or killing an attacker.

Is Aikido a religion or do practitioners follow a particular religion?
No. People of all religions practice Aikido. It is, however, a spiritual endeavor. Aikido's ethical standards enable us to develop our spiritual being and character. By interacting with our inner selves and others at the same time, Aikido brings about both internal and external peace simultaneously. It is a pursuit that denies no one and benefits everyone.

Why all the bowing?
The bowing in Aikido is done to show mutual respect, trust, and acceptance of others. It should be sincere, not mechanical.

How do I start?
Whenever you are ready, just sign up, step onto the mat, and bow. It is as simple as that.

Can I start without a gi?
Yes. Although you may feel more comfortable with a gi, you may start with loose comfortable clothing such as sweats or a warm-up outfit. We do suggest, however, that the best way to practice Aikido is with a traditional gi.

How long will it take before I "know"Aikido?
That depends on many factors. Everyone has a different temperament, different physical capabilities, and different aptitudes for learning. Some people, for example, learn mechanical technique quickly but lack the essence and true spirit needed for Aikido. Others come to Aikido with the essence already part of their character and practice integrating it with Aikido's martial techniques. It may take you years of training—or you may "know it" already. In either case, enjoy your daily practice.

How long will it take me to get a black belt?
Achieving a black belt in traditional Aikido is the most difficult of all the martial arts (a minimum of about five years of diligent practice).

How fast you progress is relative to the quality of your practice and the amount of time you put into it. It is the same with any endeavor you decide to undertake.

However, the black belt should not be a "golden calf." If you practice sincerely and open your heart, you may find you have achieved something much more valuable than a black belt. You may achieve a feeling of self-mastery in your very first class or at any moment thereafter.

I'm afraid I'll be too clumsy and get embarrassed.
Don't worry, you are not alone. We all experience clumsiness whether we are on the mat or not. It happens all the time. Tea cups spill on occasion and feet do trip on all sorts of myste-

rious objects that suddenly rise up (and sometimes completely disappear again!). If you think this doesn't happen to everyone—think again. Notice how other people handle themselves. Laugh a little at yourself at times when you feel like a "klutz," and then forget it and move on. Relax and have a good time with the newness of learning.

Will I hold back an advanced student if we train together?
Absolutely not. As you progress in Aikido it is essential to be comfortable working with both advanced students and beginners. Both have extremely valuable lessons to give you. Later, as an advanced student, it will be your responsibility to remember when you started and see yourself in others when they begin to follow you. In helping a beginner with their practice, you will be able to focus on clarifying the techniques not only to them but to yourself. This is why a teacher can say, "I learn from my students."

How will I ever learn all the Japanese terms?
Again, don't worry. Through repetition and association with the techniques, you will be surprised to find out how much you learn in only a short time.

Do I have to know Japanese to understand Aikido?
Knowing Japanese is not a prerequisite for knowing Aikido, a martial way based on being in harmony with nature and its principles. Familiarity with the Japanese language may, however, help give you better insight into Aikido's cultural roots.

Why do some students wear black skirts?
The black pleated skirt-like garment is called a *hakama*. It is a traditional Japanese garment worn in Aikido by advanced students and black belts only (some schools may allow be-

ginners or juniors to wear hakama). It has been retained in Aikido because of the way it enhances the beautiful circular movements of Aikido. On a more practical level, it hides the movements of the feet and gives the wearer a unique feeling of grounding and movement. The strapping and tying also gives an enhanced awareness of the physical center or *hara*.

Can I leave the mat during class?
Yes, you may. But please get permission from the instructor to do so first.

Can I take private lessons?
It is up to the discretion of the chief instructor. It may be difficult to truly learn Aikido in such a limiting format. Use private lessons to enhance your regular class training.

What's going on with the breathing exercises?
Drawing in a deep breath, relaxing it down into our centers, and letting it out slowly calms us, gives us fresh energy, releases tension, relaxes our shoulders, and enables us to find a comfortable, alive, natural posture. During the breathing (and the hand shaking that you see), we are gathering the energies of both heaven and earth to ourselves. We cup our hands together (palm to palm, dominant hand is generally underneath), and shake them to churn and mix the energies with our bodies and our beings. This practice helps make our center come alive.

Do the rolls and high falls hurt? I hear people slapping the mat when they fall. Does that hurt?
Sometimes when learning to fall (learning *ukemi*) some students may experience minor discomfort until they learn to

33

smooth out their ukemi. "Slapping out" does not hurt, even though it sounds like it would. "Its bark is louder than its bite" would apply here. It simply helps dissipate the energy of the roll or high fall.

Why don't you wear colored belts?
In traditional Aikido, the white belt is worn by all ranks until reaching *shodan* (the first rung of the ladder, considered only the beginning. At attaining shodan, a student is considered a serious student—not an "expert."). This de-emphasizes the importance of outward signs of rank or accomplishment and promotes a more internal awareness and introspection of personal achievement.

I understand that O Sensei was a deeply spiritual and religious man. What religion did he devote himself to?
O Sensei practiced the Shinto and Omoto-kyo religions, both of which contain beliefs in the Kotodama theory (the belief of sound creating and re-creating the universe). O Sensei based his creation of Aikido on Kotodama.

In your own Aikido practice you may come to realize that all movement and non-movement—all life—has a palpable resonance.

Please note:
When O Sensei spoke of his belief in a higher power he referred to the Japanese concept of *kami*. In simplistic terms, kami can be translated as "spirits" or akin to the western notion of "God." I must stress that the idea of kami is a very complex belief and warrants further study on the part of the serious Aikidoist in order to gain a deeper understanding of the Founder's words.

Joining a Dojo

Guidelines and Responsibilities of the Aikido Student

Membership in a traditional Aikido dojo is a gift. Through it you have the opportunity to improve your character, your health, and your life. It is a very unique membership. It goes much deeper and is much more fulfilling than belonging to any other form of sports or fitness club.

Being a member of a dojo, you are accepted for who you are. If you are accepted into a dojo and given the opportunity of learning there, you, in turn, accept the responsibilities and privileges of dojo membership.

Membership Dues

The financial responsibilities of the dojo are met exclusively with the funds brought in through the membership dues. As a member of the dojo you have also accepted the responsibility of submitting your dues on time so that the dojo can meet its financial obligations. Your membership fee is usually due on the first day of each month. Whether you intend to train every day or not at all, your membership dues should still be submitted. This will keep your membership in good standing, but, more importantly, also support the dojo you have decided to join. In other words, you do not pay your membership dues to receive instruction. You pay your membership dues in appreciation of dojo membership. It is a way to show concern for the welfare of your dojo and teacher.

Since your dues are important, be aware of when they are to be paid and submit them on time. A member of a dojo should never need a reminder to pay dues. It is an embarrassment to all involved; both to those who have to be reminded, as well as to those who are put in the awkward position of doing the reminding.

If you will not be around the dojo for an extended period of time due to traveling, vacation, injury, or other obligations, please tell your chief instructor, so a leave of absence might be granted. This is also intended as a courtesy to your chief instructor because he/she will notice if you have not been in class and instructors are sincerely concerned about you.

Personal Hygiene

Always make sure your hands, feet, and face are clean before getting onto the mat. Keep your finger- and toenails trimmed short so as not to injure yourself, your partner, or your instructor. If you have a recent cut, use a bandage or a secure band aid. If you receive a scratch or cut while practicing, leave the mat immediately, and clean and bandage it securely.

You and Your Gi

The traditional uniform for Aikido training is a gi, consisting of a white jacket, white pants, and a white *obi* (belt). The white obi is worn by all kyu ranks until reaching yudansha (black belt) level. Then a black belt is worn. In some dojos, colored belts are worn by kyu ranks to denote rank. However, this is the exception rather than the rule.

Your gi should always be clean and neat. Fold your gi after washing or practicing in it to avoid wrinkling. Never crumple or roll it into a ball. This is not the way your gi should be

SOME COMMON (& NOT SO COMMON) OBI/GI MISTAKES:

NO OBI.
NO DRAWSTRING.
PLENTY OF
LAUGHING.

NO OBI.
GI TOP TUCKED
INTO PANTS.
PANTS ON
BACKWARDS.
(DOES NOT
UNDERSTAND
THE HUMOR IN IT.)

OBI A BIT
TOO HIGH.
(KNOT
SHOULD BE
AROUND BOTH
WRAPPINGS.)

NO
COMMENT.

OBI AROUND
NECK. SPENDS
TOO MUCH TIME
AT THE OFFICE.
NICE GUCCI BELT.

OBI WRAPPED
ONLY ONCE
AROUND
THEN TIED.
(DO NOT
CORRECT WITH
SCISSORS.)

OBI
TOO TIGHT.

OBI
WAN
KENOBI

GI
STAPLED ON.
GI WRAPPED
NICE & TIGHT
- HOWEVER -
PERSON IS NOT.
(DO NOT CORRECT
THEM - INFORM
THE
AUTHORITIES.)

NEW SHODAN.
NEW HAKAMA.
BOTH NEED TO BE
TURNED AROUND
& ADJUSTED.
(HAKAMA ON
BACKWARDS -
HEAD NOT ON
STRAIGHT.)

treated. Respect and care should be shown to all things and cultivating this attitude can start with your gi. If holes or rips develop, repair them. Bleach should only be used to remove difficult stains. If your gi remains in bad condition despite the care you give it, it is time to think about getting a new one.

Wash your gi regularly. Remember the saying, "Aikido is not an offensive art." You don't want to offend anyone with your gi.

How to Wear Your Gi

Put the pants on first with the loops in front. Tighten the waist strings and tie in front. Put the jacket on next, with the left lapel over the right. If it is customary in your dojo, you should write your name on the left shoulder or lapel using a permanent marker. This makes it easier for your fellow students to remember your name. It is also advisable to label your pants and obi to prevent a mix-up. Women should wear a white tee-shirt under their gi jacket.

The best way to learn how to tie your obi is to ask a senior student. They will be happy to guide you through it.

Please note: After arriving at the dojo and putting on your gi, look around for some way you can help to take care of the dojo. Does the mat need sweeping? Do the shelves need dusting? Maybe you can help a new student tie their belt or show them how to "bow on" to the mat.

Also, after class and before you take off your gi, ask yourself once again, "What can I do to show my appreciation for the benefits I received from Aikido class?" The mat always needs to be swept, so you can take a turn with that, or look around for something else that *you* can do for *your* dojo.

The Hakama

The hakama can be worn at most Aikido dojos by men and women students after attaining shodan (first degree black belt). Some dojos may allow kyu ranks to wear a hakama. Customs and reasons vary from dojo to dojo.

The hakama has been retained in Aikido because of the aesthetic beauty it adds to the movement of Aikido. It gives the wearer an enhanced feeling of movement along with a better sense of their center. It also gives alternating floating and grounding sensations. From an ancient technical aspect, the hakama was worn to hide the movement of the feet.

If you have the privilege of wearing a hakama you must learn how to fold, wear, and care for it properly. Ask your instructor or senior students for their help and instructions. Traditionally, either a blue or black hakama should be worn. If your hakama shows sign of wear (the knees are the first to go) make plans for a new one. Full, clean gi pants are to be worn underneath— meaning no cut-offs or holes in the knees.

If you are *sempai* (senior student) or an instructor, a neat, clean appearance sets an example to the students in your charge. It is imperative that you present yourself in a suitable manner.

No Jewelry on the Mat

Aikido training requires that you remove all jewelry, including but not limited to watches, necklaces, chains, earrings, bracelets, and *all* rings. This is for your own safety, the safety of your fellow students and your instructor, and the safety of your valuables.

Keeping the Dojo Clean

It is every member's responsibility to the keep dojo and mat clean. This means before and after every class, sweeping, dusting and vacuuming should be done. If you possess these skills, your dojo needs you!

This request goes out to all students of all levels in all dojos. How do you know if you should help? When on the mat, look down. If you see a gi and bare feet, odds are you are a clean-up volunteer.

Here are some clean-up guidelines:

- After each and every class everyone (especially seniors) should grab a broom and sweep the mat while someone gets the vacuum.

- The areas in front of the kamiza and where the instructor bows in should be done first. Sweeping should be done away from those areas—never towards them. (Sweeping should never end in these areas because of the chance of leaving missed dirt behind. This does not show proper respect for the kamiza or the sensei who will be bowing into a field of debris.

- All rugs and floors should be kept clean and vacuumed.

- Bathroom sinks, toilets, etc. need to be kept clean.

- Dressing rooms should be kept neat and cleaned daily.

- All litter should be picked up and discarded.

- The kamiza, walls, furniture, counters, shelves, stairways, windows, mirrors, and all flat surfaces should be cleaned and dusted on a regular basis.

- Dojos with vinyl mat covers should be wiped down as often as possible to keep them clean and germ-free.

- Along with the mat and kamiza, all areas of the dojo should be checked and cleaned daily.

- If there are plants in the dojo, they should be cared for and watered regularly.

Every member of the dojo should be concerned about these matters. Keeping yourself and your facility clean can and should be a valuable part of the dojo experience. Always take your turn with the broom, mop, vacuum, and dust cloth and take a few minutes on occasion to help with other chores around the dojo. Senior students, in particular, should set a good example.

Cleaning, maintenance, and occasional special projects (preparing mailings, assisting with repairs and renovations, etc.) are also the responsibility of every member of the dojo.

Remember—it is *your* dojo. It is your obligation and responsibility to keep it clean and safe.

Special Projects

The dojo is kept running and in good repair by the efforts of the students. It is the ongoing result of a cooperative effort. Everyone combines their talents in order to better the dojo. Carpenters, electricians, plumbers, lawyers, printers, and artists all come together and volunteer their professional abilities. Everyone is encouraged to contribute their thoughts and ideas to help the dojo. If you would like to contribute your knowledge and abilities in helping your dojo, please mention it to your instructor. They will be most appreciative.

If a special project is announced, try to help, even if you can help only a little bit. "Many hands make light work." You will not only better the dojo, but you will also help others who are volunteering. You will gain satisfaction while having a good time with your friends.

Use of the Dojo

The Aikido dojo is just that—a dojo for the practice of Aikido. It is not to be used for any other purpose or practice of any other martial art, without the express permission of the chief instructor. Use of the dressing rooms, bathrooms, lounges, kitchen areas, etc., should reflect the same respect and awareness shown on the mat.

ng In

The majority of dojos require that you sign in or mark an attendance sheet. This is a record of the classes you have attended, referred to prior to any promotion test to verify that you have fulfilled the time requirements.

If you visit another dojo, attend a seminar, or take a private lesson with a certified instructor, you may be able to mark it on the appropriate day on your home dojo attendance sheet. If you travel and train at a dojo elsewhere, you may be able to mark that in at your home dojo as well.

Valuables

Valuables can sometimes be stored safely during class with the instructor, who will either hold them in the office area or indicate to you a safe place in which to store them. This includes jewelry, wallets, watches, large amounts of cash, or, in the case of law enforcement officers, firearms. Feel free to ask your instructor for permission to take advantage of this service. Ultimately, the safety of your valuables is your responsibility. Exercise care, not carelessness.

Seminars

As part of your Aikido training, it is recommended that you experience a wide variety of qualified teachers since each one is unique in their style and approach. They may give new insights and ways of looking at your technique. Because it is difficult for the average student to travel and experience other inspirational Aikido teachers, your dojo may sponsor periodic seminars to bring those teachers to their students.

Often a dojo will sponsor special one- or two-day Aikido seminars throughout the year. Usually a highly respected and gifted guest instructor is invited especially for the occasion.

Most often there is an additional, modest fee for attending. This is necessary because a great deal of time, effort, and expense is involved in putting a seminar together. Energy and smiles are usually in abundance at Aikido seminars. All levels, beginners and advanced, can benefit. So, please, show your support, for your benefit and the dojo's.

Seminars are also a chance for students from various dojos to get together. Sometimes there is a potluck party afterwards where students can relax and visit with each other.

The real value of seminars, though, is in the instruction that students receive. Students who attend seminars will find that their practice improves dramatically whether they attend just a couple of classes or all of them.

Testing may be included at seminars. If you are testing, your attendance (unless given special permission by your instructor) is usually mandatory. This is so your general practice can be observed and evaluated.

When a seminar is announced, volunteer yourself to your instructor to help to whatever degree you are able. Offer to help prepare the dojo or to clean up afterwards. Whatever time you can give will be greatly appreciated.

Seminars may be scheduled for one evening, one or two days, and on occasion three or more days.

Attending Class

Punctuality is essential in the dojo as well as in our daily lives. The opening ceremony and warm up for each class is important, so please be on time.

Take a few minutes before class begins to sit quietly on the mat in *seiza* (see page 47). Position yourself at the edge of the mat, facing the kamiza, in preparation for bowing in. Use this time to relax your mind and body, forget the day's pressures, and prepare for the class to come.

Observing Class

You may observe a class any time. In fact, you can gain a different perspective by doing so. If you are resting an injury, for example, you are always welcome and encouraged to watch a class.

While observing, remain unobtrusive and respectful. Do not talk to anyone on the mat without first getting the permission of the instructor. Refrain from speaking when class is beginning or closing, or when the instructor is demonstrating for the class. It is a privilege to watch, so respect the concentration of your fellow students on the mat and be quiet. If visitors enter the dojo, it would be appreciated and most helpful to the instructor if you would make them welcome, show them where they can sit, and give them the appropriate literature. Be cordial and courteous. Remember, you represent the dojo.

Visiting Other Dojos

When visiting other dojos be aware that they may have particular rules and ways of doing things. Keep an open mind and receive the instruction offered there with sincere gratitude. Be respectful and show your best manners. Remember, you represent your dojo, and your instructor as well.

To summarize, here are the ten most important things you should always keep in mind as a member of the dojo:

1. Have fun!

2. Always pay your membership dues on time at the beginning of the month.

3. Do your part in helping to keep the dojo clean.

4. Treat others with courtesy, kindness, and sincere respect.

5. Make sure your hands and feet are clean before stepping onto the mat. Keep your fingernails and toenails trimmed for safety.

6. Keep your gi clean and neat. Wash it regularly and fold it neatly. (You may print your first name on your left lapel or upper left sleeve as well as your obi and pants).

7. Remove *all* jewelry before stepping on the mat. (Ask your instructor for a safe place to keep it while you are training.)

8. When you step on the mat, give either a standing or kneeling bow in the direction of the kamiza. If class is already in session, wait by the edge of the mat until the instructor waves you onto the mat. Then bow to the instructor, step onto the mat, and bow toward the kamiza. In most cases, only the chief instructors need to be addressed as Sensei. All other Junior and Assistant Instructors may be addressed by their first names.

9. Sign in on the attendance sheet when you arrive for class.

10. Like anything worth learning, Aikido also takes time and practice. Don't worry about being awkward—as a beginner, it is only natural. If you have any questions, comments or concerns, feel free to talk to your instructor or the senior students. They will be happy to help you.

Special note:

Iaido ("live" sword drawing)

Iaido is an entirely separate martial art from Aikido. However, some Aikido teachers feel it enhances the practice of Aikido.

Benefits include enhanced focusing, a meditative, relaxed, and open mind, better balance, and grounding in conjunction with powerful extension while cutting. The cuts of a live blade, as in Iaido, differ somewhat from the cuts used in Aiki-ken (Aikido swordsmanship). The basic footwork in Iaido is also generally different from Aiki-ken and Aikido foot movements. If you practice both Aikido and Iaido, be aware of the differences and keep a clear distinction between the two arts.

Iaido should only be practiced with the permission of the chief instructor, under proper supervision at an established time.

A serious atmosphere is created when an individual is practicing his or her Iaido. Therefore, when watching, be mindful of this and show respect to the person's practice by giving them a quiet space and keeping your distance. Do not interrupt their practice and do not step onto the mat. Finally, never come within ten feet of someone practicing with a sword—and especially never approach them from the back. This can cause serious injury.

Etiquette

"Aikido is the way of calling people together and reconciling them with love whenever they may attack us. When they angrily attack, smilingly reconcile them. This is the true way of Aikido."

—*Morihei Ueshiba*

GOOD MANNERS ARE important in the dojo as well as in daily life. We show others respect and common courtesy through our actions. Our actions should reflect what is in our hearts and minds. Furthermore, if we act courteously to someone yet we are insincere, they can tell, just as we can determine someone else's insincerity. Strive to develop a true feeling of respect, courtesy, and friendship to all, whether inside or outside the dojo.

The two proper methods of sitting on the mat are in seiza or, if you are unable to sit in seiza, crosslegged "Indian style."

Seiza (Formal sitting posture):

Sit on your heels with big toes touching or crossed right over left. Your knees should be about two fists apart. Your palms rest on top of the thighs with your elbows relaxed against your sides. Maintain a comfortable erect posture.

Bowing

The most obvious form of dojo etiquette is bowing. After entering the dojo and removing our

 shoes, we give a standing bow to the practice space. This bow is to the spirit of those that came before us, to those who will come after us, to the spirit of O Sensei, and to give thanks for the art, the practice area, and the opportunity to train in it. (This is also a good time to check to see if you have indeed removed your shoes! Also, removing your hat after entering the dojo is a universal sign of good etiquette.)

The bow is not a religious formality, it is a gesture of respect. Aikido is not a religion, but it is definitely a spiritual undertaking.

Proper Bowing from Seiza

A kneeling bow from seiza starts with good posture. Begin the bow by placing your left hand flat on the mat followed by your right, forming a triangle with your thumbs and forefingers. Then bow, keeping good posture. Your elbows lightly touch the outside of your knees while in the bow. The triangle formed by your hands is then in front of your face. This protects the nose from injury should your head be pushed down. Unlike bows practiced in other martial arts where you keep your eyes on your opponent, the Aikido bow allows you to lower your head and gaze, taking your eyes off the person to whom you are bowing. This not only shows the most respect and trust, but helps to develop *zanshin,* intuitive awareness, and the perceptions of the other senses as well.

Standing Bow

Standing with feet together, arms at your sides, bow slightly from the waist.

"Bowing On"

When stepping onto the mat, bow again in the direction of the shomen (or kamiza) to give acknowledgement, respect, and thanks to the practice area (the mat) and the spirit and memory of the founder of Aikido. This bow is usually done from the seiza position.

If class is already in session, stand or sit in seiza near the edge of the mat and watch for the instructor to give you permission to enter the class and step onto the mat. Once you are acknowledged, give a short bow. After stepping onto the mat give a standing or sitting bow. Be sure to stretch and warm-up at the edge of the mat before joining in the practice.

As Class Is about to Start

The last five minutes before class should be a time of quiet preparation. Sit calmly in meditation or do gentle stretching, being mindful of those around you who are also seeking a peaceful state of mind before class begins. If you must talk to someone, keep it at a whisper. Two minutes before class, everyone should be sitting quietly in line ready for the start of class.

"Lining Up" for Class

Kamiza

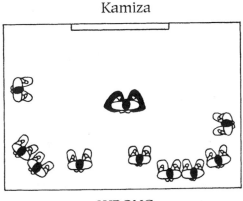

WRONG

Kamiza

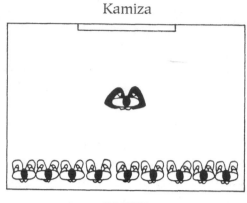

RIGHT

"Bowing In"

Students should line up in close ranks facing the kamiza along the edge of the mat. In most Aikido dojos the traditional lining up according to rank is not necessary.

The instructor first leads the class in bowing to the kamiza. Then the instructor turns and bows to the students, who in return bow to him/her. *"Onegaishimasu"* is said at this time.

Bowing during Class

After the warm-up and demonstration of the first partner practice technique, bow to the person next to you and begin practice. If the instructor calls for a change of partners, bow to your present partner and thank him/her. Then find and bow to a new partner before beginning your practice together.

Bowing to Your Partner

Bowing is an acknowledgement of the responsibility to care for others during practice. With the bow, partners agree to be responsible for each other. This understanding is an agreement of honor and should be practiced accordingly.

If your obi needs to be retied or your gi comes undone, the most polite etiquette dictates that you go to the edge of the mat and either sit in seiza or stand and face away from the kamiza while fixing your gi or obi. When finished you can once again give a short bow to your partner to resume practice.

If your partner's gi comes undone take a seat in seiza at the edge of the mat next to them and facing the kamiza. When they are ready to resume practice, bow to them and take your place on the mat once again.

If your partner has to stop his/her practice for a longer period of time, whether to catch his/her breath or leave the mat for some reason, you may ask permission from students practicing nearby to work in threes with them until your partner returns. When your partner is able to resume practicing, bow to the pair you were working with and thank them before returning to your partner.

Bowing to the Instructor

If the instructor helps you with your practice, thank them while giving a standing bow when they have finished.

If the instructor is helping someone next to you and you wish to observe, take a seated position safely out of the way and again give a bow of thanks when they have finished.

When the instructor calls you out to help demonstrate in front of the class (in other words, "to take ukemi" [see page 63]), give either a kneeling bow (if you are already kneeling) or a standing bow (if you are already standing) to the instructor. Move quickly to help the instructor. When the instructor finishes the demonstration, give a kneeling bow from seiza, then return to your partner.

If the instructor calls out and/or claps to change techniques or to clarify the present practice, line up at the edge of the mat quickly and pay immediate attention to what is being said or demonstrated. Be quiet so as not to disturb others so they may also concentrate on the words and movements of the instructor.

"Bowing Out"

At the end of class the students straighten their gis and line up. The instructor then leads the class in a bow in the same manner as "bowing in." At this time, the instructor thanks the students with a seated bow and the students respond likewise with a bow from seiza to finish class. The class may respond with either a "Thank you, Sensei," or *"Domo Arigato Gozaimashita, Sensei!"*

"Bowing Off" the Mat

After class remember to bow again towards the kamiza before stepping off of the mat.

Upon leaving the dojo, it is once again proper to give a short standing bow to the dojo space.

"Bowing On" at Seminars

At seminars, it is generally not necessary to wait for the instructor's permission to step on the mat and enter the class. In this case it is considered distracting to the instructor. Simply step onto the mat from the rear and "bow on" in as quiet and unobtrusive a manner as possible so as not to disturb the instructor or the other students. Be aware that these rules for "bowing on" vary slightly from one dojo to another as well as one seminar to another. You may be required to wait for the instructor's acknowledgement if class has already begun.

One Final Note

In terms of etiquette, when in doubt, always be thoughtful, courteous, and polite.

Training in Aikido

*"Practice at all times with a feeling of pleasurable ex-
hilaration."*

excerpt from: "Rules During Practice"
posted at Aikido World Headquarters, Tokyo

Notes for the Beginner

First of all, let yourself relax and have a good time. It is nor-
mal to be nervous. Everyone you see in the dojo has gone
through exactly the same thing. For everyone—even the sensei—there was a day when they first stepped onto the mat
as a beginner. If frustration arises, talk to the instructor or
your fellow students. Remember, everyone is there to learn
together.

The paramount rule when training in Aikido is to have respect and courtesy for the other people in the dojo. Respect
and courtesy is given not only to the instructors and sempai
but to all others—the junior students *(kohai)* who follow you,
visitors to the dojo, or anyone you may meet for the rest of
your life.

An atmosphere of cooperation—not competition—is called
for. Cooperation literally means, "in Aikido, we are here to
help each other." This does not mean you must "give in" to
another person's will, as some tend to think. It means we learn
to *operate together.* This is necessary because the techniques
in Aikido can have terrible ramifications if not practiced in
the proper manner. Severe injury can occur to yourself, your
partner, or others on the mat if you are not mindful and care-

53

ful. Therefore, after experiencing the effectiveness of Aikido yourself, you should then practice sincerely with compassion and full awareness.

A true Aikidoist wishes to do no harm to anyone and prefers a peaceful resolution to any conflict. Therefore, skills developed in sensing trouble and avoiding it are preferred over the option of using the martial abilities one has developed. Sensitivity to situations and trust in instinct and intuition become the Aikidoist's best tools. These qualities are honed on the mat every time you begin working with your partner. In other words, practice not only the technique that was demonstrated but also "tune in to where your partner is at" and sense their state of mind and being.

Remember: If you become frustrated or confused, don't hesitate to talk to your instructor or fellow students. They will be very happy to try and help.

The Role of Seniors (Sempai)

Helping the First Day Student

Seniors should take the initiative to make friends with new students and make them feel at home. Show them how to put on their gi, tie their obi, how to bow onto the mat, and be ready to assist them during warm-ups.

Sempai, who are given the privilege and responsibility of guiding a beginner through his/her first days in the dojo, should give new students a positive experience. Show kindness and patience. Through you, the new student is about to get his/her first impressions of Aikido, the quality of the dojo, and your true character. Remember, you never get a second chance to make a first impression. If you show you care and show them what they can do (not what they can't), you go a long way to opening a whole new world to them.

Helping Junior Students

Seniors should help juniors (kohai) with sincerity. They should show and feel true concern in guiding them. They should not use this opportunity as a chance to preach, give a long-winded speech, or demonstrate how much they "know" (and how little the junior knows). When helping others on the mat, we must all overcome the tendency to be too verbal. Mat time is practice time. Talking too much is a mistake. Keep your words brief and to the point. Although in the western world we are used to learning through verbal instruction, the real learning in Aikido comes from experiencing it.

You should allow students to complete their technique. They will become frustrated and resentful if you constantly stop their attempts at techniques. They are learning what makes a technique effective and if you stop them from experiencing and expressing it for themselves you make true learning nearly impossible. When you make it too difficult for them to practice their technique, or stop it before it can get started, they instinctively want to use other options and are not encouraged to keep to the practice at hand. Guide them through their technique with your ukemi—letting them feel their specific response to the prescribed attack. As they grasp the basic technique, how it relates to a specific attack, and its ukemi, they are then able to begin working on changes and variables as well as increased resistance and intensity.

So, when you are helping someone, keep the talking to a minimum, be patient, and show kindness. Let them practice and learn. Let them experience the difficulty, the joy, and the value that comes from their own discovery. Your partner will appreciate it and think better of you for it. If your words are condescending and your attitude is bad, or you stop their attempts at technique, don't expect to make a friend. Treat them as you would like to be treated and you will not only get their attention but their respect and friendship as well.

Senior students should always set a good example in demeanor, etiquette, practice, cleaning and care of the dojo, personal appearance, and ability to smile.*

To Gi or Not to Gi

For those times when you need motivation . . .

Tough day at work? Too much on your mind? Feeling kind of down? No energy? Too busy?

All good reasons not to take class today, right?

WRONG! These are all excellent reasons to pack a gi and get down to the dojo!

As soon as you decide to do that, your day will change. Maybe just a little bit, maybe a lot. By the time you have packed your gi and are on the way to the dojo, your own personal ritual for transformation has begun. The drive to the dojo, for instance, can be used to process the day and "let go" of it. With each step, let your problems drop away. Each door you close behind you separates you from the difficulties of the day. Changing from your street clothes to your gi can be a particularly effective tool. Troubles can be "removed" with

---

*For further reading, with respect to beginners and sempai guidelines, see: "Rules During Practice," pp. 174–176 in *Aikido* by Kisshomaru Ueshiba (Tokyo: Kodansha, 1974) and "Rules for Beginners / Rules for Instructors," pp. 170–192 in *Aikido in Daily Life* by Koichi Tohei (Tokyo: Rikugei, 1966).

your clothes and a "fresh new you" stepped into when you put on your gi. By the time you reach the mat, whether you are aware of it or not, the transformation has already begun. If you could check, you would probably find such changes as lowered blood pressure, tense muscles relaxing, and brain wave patterns moving from a heightened BETA state to a more relaxing ALPHA state. Take notice next time you sit down on the mat. Take a deep breath and feel the difference. Then let your breath be soft and from your belly, "like a baby." When you have this feeling going into class, you will maximize the quality of your time on the mat. Keep it while working on technique, and you will be working on relaxing while at the same time stimulating both body and mind.

During practice you should touch and be touched in a way that builds cooperation, compassion, and a sense of protection. This is because the quality of the touch that Aikido develops is very unique. While making physical connections with your partners, you are also "tuning in" to their spirits. You feel their hearts and, in the process, open yours. This kind of touch can create and receive powerful healing on physical, emotional, and spiritual levels. This is available whenever you practice Aikido in the proper spirit.

The benefits of Aikido training are so numerous, so varied and far reaching that they can never be adequately listed or described. So the next time you are debating whether to go to class, think about what a difference it will make.

Because of its depth, complexity, and variety, Aikido is not an easy path, but the friends you make, the exhilaration you will feel, and the positive changes it will bring about in your life will make it a lot easier.

Remember—keep an open mind, remind yourself to relax, and have a good time.

Practice and Forget

Don't worry about committing everything to memory. The repetition of the techniques in daily practice will take care of that.

New students are often overwhelmed with all the techniques and new information. It is very difficult to commit it all to memory.

When you read a book, for instance, you can recall more easily the specifics of what you have just read. It would be quite difficult to repeat the entire book word for word. However, you would know what the book was about and understand the entire story. Approach your training in the same way. It is a journey. Each class is a special chapter of its own.

Through varied repetition, all the basic techniques will become ingrained. We practice the basics with a wide range of attacks in order to find their commonality. The essence of these basics can then be applied universally in response to any attack. Techniques may be very different but always look for the common strategy.

First Day and Every Day

Train with a spirit of open exhilaration and take each class as the brand new experience it is. The old adage of "you never step into the same river twice" comes to mind. The water you touched last step is gone and new water takes its place. The force of the current constantly changes. Even the river bed foundation perpetually erodes and is replaced.

You are not exactly the same person you were in your last class and neither is anyone else—including the instructor. Even if you practiced the same techniques at the last class, conditions are always different and entirely new insight is gained.

We are dynamic, ever-changing, complex individuals in ever-changing environments of weather, temperature, stress, temperament, emotions, and degrees of healthiness. You are an individual created anew every time you open your eyes in the morning. You face a new day with new opportunities and challenges. You entertain both negative and positive outlooks and you must constantly choose one or the other. One can be debilitating and draining, sapping you of precious life energy. The other can provide you with a life force that is fresh and continually revitalizing. It will lift you up beyond the difficulties that come your way. Make no mistake about it—you do have a choice.

Warm-Up

Class always begins with a series of stretching, breathing and warm-up exercises to prepare us for training. All of these exercises have valuable significance and not only prepare your body, but your mind and senses as well. They should be performed with full attention in order to bring your mind and body into balance. If the warm-up is approached in the proper manner, an awareness (zanshin) will open up naturally. A centering will result which can then be carried into the practice that follows.

The Posture of Aikido

In most aikido dojos, the stance one adopts is a natural one. It allows us to move easily and quickly in any direction. It is a comfortable relaxed stance *(hanmi)* which takes the form of a triangle. (Some Aikido styles still use a *kamae,* or ready fighting stance. It is similar to holding a sword in front of the body with the palms open and forward and the fingers outstretched.)

Since, in Aikido, we do not have the intention to fight, our posture, stance, and mental attitude should reflect that state. The stance is open, the chest and gut being the open receptor of any information. We allow this information to come in, just as we allow in the attack and the attacker. When we adapt a fighting stance, we cut off that important visceral intuitive information. We show that we are expecting a fight. Our adversary is forewarned and now expects a fight even if one was not intended.

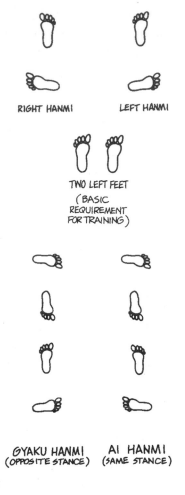

The arms and hands/fists coming up in an "on guard" position act as a shield and ironically show our fear of the confrontation. The attacker then sharpens his awareness and may try to hide his true attack.

With the open receptive stance and posture of modern Aikido we show no malice. We are non-threatening. We are calm, in balance, and better able to see and understand all that the situation brings with it. In this non-stance, we are fully aware. We are relaxed and ready to respond appropriately to any situation. We emit a courageousness that can be quite compelling, without being intimidating.

We stay open and let the attacker feel he/she can come in unchallenged and full of confidence. The person might think, "Oh, great!" and come in for the kill, expecting no resistance and complete victory. Their intention is clear, as are their actions. In this way they are easily perceived, avoided, and dispatched.

To go further, when we assume a fighting stance we separate ourselves from our attacker. Aikido, ideally, is about coming together. It is about reconciliation and the recognition that we are all part of the same whole. With an open stance you recognize and feel the shared oneness. You can literally feel the truth—no separation. You allow the other person in. They are, after all, already within us. Recognize this and you realize you are in the other already as well. If you think about it, there is much more that connects us to everything and everyone than separates us.

Many martial ways teach people how to fight effectively. Some arts even attract people who like to fight. Aikido is for people who prefer not to fight but can and will defend themselves with appropriateness at least, and with benevolence and love at best.

The posture one develops in Aikido is one that does not have to listen—it hears; does not have to look—it sees; does not have to ask—it knows; does not have to hate—it loves.

△ ○ □

The symbols associated with Aikido are the triangle, circle, and square. Many interesting and valuable explanations are available for these symbols and what they represent in Aikido.

In abbreviated terms I offer the following associations:

△ symbolizes entering and harmonizing. Like the bow of a ship cutting through water.

○ symbolizes blending, including inhaling and redirecting. Similar to the hurricane, tremendous power is in its spinning vortex, yet its center remains calm.

□ symbolizes stability, exhaling, and grounding. Aikido begins and ends with a strong, steady, balanced foundation.

Falling in Aikido
(or "The Other Half of Your Practice")

Falling does not mean failure in Aikido. It means adjusting to a situation and going with the flow—keeping your center and adjusting to a situation, maintaining yourself, and surviving a technique in a safe and unruffled manner. The title of a book by Terry Dobson, a respected Aikido teacher and student of O Sensei, says it well: *Giving In to Get Your Way* (re-released as *Aikido In Everyday Life* by North Atlantic Books).

Rather than looking at the mat as a symbol of defeat or as something to be avoided, welcome it. Make friends with it so you will enjoy each time you return to it. Respect its nature and work with it, just as you do with any other practice partner. After all, it is the mat that allows you to return to an upright and balanced state.

Ukemi

When "taking ukemi" (giving the attack and absorbing the throw) give a clear strong attack with a clear mind. Then, once you feel your attack being redirected do not resist it. Rather, blend with the technique fully and ride it like a wave. It is only when you hang back or lag behind the technique that injury, either physical or emotional, is likely to occur.

Remember the old story about the oak tree that resisted the wind and snapped, and the willow that yielded to it and survived, springing back to its original state. Flexibility and the ability to adjust are attributes that help body and mind, the work environment, and even good government. Good Aikido requires it.

Here is another example: on the mat, which would you rather be? The one who, by not moving with a technique, receives its full power? Or the one who does not resist the full power of a technique but moves with it in full confidence, rolling and returning once again to balance?

THEODORE STILL NEEDS TO WORK ON HIS ABILITY
TO FOLLOW

Atemi Waza (Striking Techniques)

Atemi waza are feigned strikes used to unbalance or distract the opponent. Of course, the atemi can be fully delivered but the true skill is in accomplishing the technique without having to resort to that extreme. Some teachers stress atemi waza strongly, others never use it or even refer to it. Both approaches have their merit.

When delivering atemi waza, always use caution and control. Atemi waza however, should never distract you from the true purpose and flow of the technique being practiced.

Breathing

In the buzzing pace of the day, how often do you pay attention to the rising and falling of your breath? Probably only when you are short of it after some form of exertion. As with many valuable things in our life that we tend to take for granted until they are leaving us or have gone altogether, it is the same with our Breath (I capitalize it to stress its importance). Seldom do we acknowledge its importance to us. Each time we draw a Breath we draw Life—our life, given to us every moment. Take notice once in a while and be thankful for it.

We begin each class by doing just that. This is the time we take to savor the sweetness of our Breathing. During our warm-up we focus on how it makes our actions possible. We strive to integrate it with our movements, gaining a fuller appreciation and knowledge of our bodies.

In your Breathing exercises, draw in the Breath through your nose. Let it settle in your lower belly a moment and return it through your mouth. Your Breathing should be natural, not be excessively loud or labored.

While inhaling, feel the life energy fill your body and being—a gift from all there is. Draw it in not only through your nose but through your fingers and hands, the soles of your feet, the crown of your head, and with every pore of your body. Exhale with the same attention and awareness, returning the Breath in the same manner. Now, awake and alive with life energy, move on.

Breathing during Training

We must coordinate our Breathing with the ebb and flow of all that is around us. This is our practice on the mat. When receiving the attack we draw in our Breath. While doing so we draw the essence of the attack into our very existence. We allow it to enter as deeply as our breath and to *be* with us. After enveloping the attack and permitting it to be part of us, we send it safely on as our Breath leaves.

Having used the Breath to draw in the attack, we can then use it to change the attack's energy. We mix it in our belly with the goodness in us and send it on its way refreshed and renewed, having passed through the depths of our inner compassion and love. A change in the attack, the attacker, and the one attacked is inevitable.

If you find yourself struggling with a technique, take notice if it causes you to hold your breath. If you allow your breath to be locked, your mind will be locked as well.

Consciously relax and open your Breath. Avoid "the fight," but maintain your right to be. Once again settle your Breath to your lower belly and let your energy flow from there. It will automatically and effortlessly show you the way to go. Listen to what your Breath tells you. It may say "extend more" or "take another route." It may say "back off," or remind you to simply move your body to regain comfort and successfully complete the technique without effort.

The more we listen to our Breathing, the easier everything becomes, both inside and outside the dojo.

Working in Pairs

In an average Aikido class we take turns being attacker *(uke)* and defender *(nage)*. Usually we practice the techniques four times, alternating right and left. Then we switch and our partner takes a turn.

Sometimes at seminars (or at some dojos) we practice the techniques only twice, (once on the right, once on the left), and then switch with our partner. This is done when, for instance, the instructor is showing a wide variety of techniques and there is only enough time (between demonstrations) for each person to quickly practice it twice. These times are rare, however, and we almost always practice the technique four times each, back and forth, until the instructor either calls for the class to change partners or change the technique.

Normally we keep the same partner until the "change partners" announcement is given, but in some dojos it is customary to change partners with every new technique or every new demonstration by the teacher.

The basic distance between partners *(ma-ai)* is one where each partner can touch only the other's fingertips with outstretched hands. This is a safe distance because, in order for either to attack, they must close the distance.

Working in Threes

It is sometimes necessary, if the mat is too crowded or there is an odd number of students on the mat, to practice in threes. This allows two people to practice while the third waits for his or her turn.

This is done in the following manner:

If you are the third person, take a seat by the edge of the mat while your other two partners begin their practice.

The beginning pair takes turns practicing the technique

twice. After the second partner has done their technique twice, the first sits down at the mat's edge. You rise and act as attacker twice for the partner left standing. Then you practice your technique twice with that person. After that, they sit down and you practice your techniques twice more with the first person. After you take ukemi twice for them, sit down and wait for your next turn.

Working in Groups

When the mat is crowded and a technique requires a lot of room to perform, the instructor may call for group practice.

The students divide themselves into groups of three or more and space themselves around the edge of the mat. The senior student in the group goes out onto the mat and faces the edge, while the others line up there. The first person in line comes out and performs the attack while the senior practices the technique.

The senior practices that technique with each person in the line, one after another. When the student first in line once again faces the senior, they bow to each other. The first person in line then takes the senior's place, and he/she goes to the end of the line. The practice proceeds in the same manner until everyone in line has had a turn practicing the technique with all the students.

A Shared Responsibility

"Do unto others as you would have them do unto you."

On the mat we get immediate feedback when we neglect the trust our partner placed in us with the first bow. If we cannot feel this feedback with our hands or see it with our eyes, we can sense it viscerally, in our gut. Whether we choose to ignore this valuable information is of great consequence, since we eventually reap the harvest of our own decisions and actions both inside and outside of the dojo.

In the atmosphere of the dojo we agree to protect each other and practice safely. This is not to say that we should practice softly or gingerly. We must experience vigorous, effective technique if we are to stay awake and fully present. Experiencing such technique, at the hands of someone we trust, is how we learn to adjust quickly and survive potentially dangerous interactions. But we should maintain the same correctness and concern regardless of the pace or level of practice. Nage and uke each share responsibility for making the technique safe so both can hone their skills in intense, rigorous training.

Those who habitually disregard the well-being of others and cause them harm are weak people with weak hearts, no matter how strong they appear physically. Those who follow the way of bullies and cowards are admired only by those of the same mind. Such people are distrusted, disliked, and perhaps even hated by others.

Those who care for others in their practice and in their lives earn friendship, respect, and love. This is the way of a true warrior—one who is fully aware of the implications of his or her actions.

If someone is working with you in an irresponsible manner, don't think, "Well, I just have to put up with this and take it." Make your partner aware of what is happening. Speak up. It is your responsibility as their training partner to help make them conscious of what they are doing. Like you, they have come to Aikido to learn how to avoid hurting others. They will most certainly appreciate it, make their apologies, and thank you.

Enjoying the Climb

Approach your training as you would climb a mountain, one step at a time. Keep comfortable and enjoy each new level. Breath deeply and fully and feel the exhilaration of being alive. Take a look around every once in a while. Look at where you were before, and at the real progress you have made. When looking at "how far you have to go," do not be discouraged. Discouragement is something you wave at but do not invite in.

When climbing a mountain, it is difficult to see the actual summit. Many times what you think is the summit turns out to be just another ridgeline when you reach it, and the summit seems as far away as before. Take heart. Whether you realize it or not, real progress has been made. Keep going steadily and enjoy the view, it gets better all the time. There will be a moment when you realize you have reached the summit, your goal. Then, to quote Dag Hammarskjold, "only when you climb a mountain and have stood on its peak can you fully realize how small it really is."

This is not to say you should not set goals. Just don't be overwhelmed by them and remain aware of the possibilities beyond. Climbing a mountain is not an easy thing to do, so enjoy the journey and have perseverance. Aikido is as exhilarating and demanding. Congratulate yourself, because you reach a summit every time you step on the mat.

Returning to the Foot of the Mountain

In order to become an experienced mountain climber you must climb again and again. Once having reached a summit you must return once again to where you started.

So it is with Aikido training. Having reached some proficiency, you must constantly return to the basics, work with fresh beginners and juniors, and keep a humble yet curious attitude in your practice. Return again and again to a fresh "beginner's mind," that precious state where all possibilities are wondrous.

The Real Value of Aikido Training

"Have you ever used it?!"

Even though Aikido is a powerful method of defending ourselves against a physical attack, the odds that we may be physically attacked are rather small. We may never have to face that situation. If we are not so lucky, maybe we will encounter it once or twice in a lifetime. If you find yourself facing trouble more often, it may be wise to take a good look at your environment, your attitude, and/or your lifestyle and change them.

The real value of Aikido training is apparent in our everyday interactions and state of being. You may find that you do indeed "use it" very often. Aikido builds your character and allows you to better interact with anyone and anything, including that voice inside bent on leading you into a poor decision or down the wrong road.

The Spirit of Practice

According to Aikido's ideals and ethics, merely practicing with the idea of defeating or injuring your partner is unacceptable. You should protect your partner with benevolence and reverence for their well-being and look for an outcome that is mutually beneficial. With Aikido you don't have to fight. You can allow your partner to complete the attack, protect yourself, and finish your technique in a manner that returns both of you to a peaceful state.

When facing an attacker we learn to empathize with him/her and we recognize that we, too, have lost our temper at times. We admit we have regretted our words or actions at some time, or acted hastily without thought to the consequences. By seeing ourselves in our attacker we "feel" for him or her. We understand his/her feelings because we know that we have such feelings as well. The other person could just be having a bad day, or to quote one of my students, "maybe even a *really* bad day."

This awareness is essential for your progress in Aikido. For a technique to be performed skillfully, it is not enough that it is technically correct. It must also display and embody compassion and love for each person. This kind of inner strength is profoundly powerful. With it you become the greatest of warriors—a warrior of peace.

Peaceful Warriors and Warrior Healers

Aikido can be practiced by many types of people for many reasons, at many levels and degrees of intensity. Whether we realize it or not we are all drawn by the real power behind Aikido—peace.

The first thing we learn to recognize is that we can easily defeat someone with the techniques of Aikido. Realizing this and having the confidence in the simple soft power of Aikido, the next stage is to see ourselves in our attacker. We must recognize our commonality and admit that we, too, have lost our balance as this person has, and perhaps have regretfully done harm to someone. We lovingly forgive the attack and the attacker while taking care that we are not injured or unbalanced by their loss of balance.

This way of approaching interactions transforms our daily life. There is conflict only if we agree that there is conflict. If we mistreat everyone we come in contact with, especially those who put their trust in us, we will have an army of people looking to mistreat us in return. If we care for and protect those we come into contact with, we will have an army of people who will care for and protect us. Be mindful, though: if selfishness is your sole motivation, that will taint the energy involved in the interaction. You must care for and give to others without ulterior motives. You should do it because it is the right thing to do. It is the way of truly powerful, peaceful people.

Weapons Training—Boken and Jo

"Standing before the enemy,
he strikes
but I am already behind him."
—Morihei Ueshiba

"To fight and conquer in one hundred battles is not the
highest skill. To subdue the enemy with no fight at all, that's
the highest skill."

—Sun Tzu

WEAPONS TRAINING IN Aikido is unique. Training with the boken (two-handed wooden long sword) is referred to as *aiki-ken* training, while training with the jo (a 52- to 54-inch wooden staff) is referred to as *aiki-jo* training. Training with these weapons has some similarities to and some differences from traditional sword and staff methods. O Sensei, having studied both, as well as other arts and weaponry, evolved them to specifically enhance Aikido training.

Weapons training teaches us how to move and use our bodies when striking, parrying, and evading. It teaches us how to keep our hands and elbows in front of and in coordination with our hips.

Aiki-ken and aiki-jo practice relate directly to actual hand-to-hand techniques, and also teach the Aikido student about distance, timing, footwork, extension, and much more. Partner practice with boken and jo also teaches us how to deal with the fear factor, and how to keep our spirits steady and strong despite the distractions of danger.

When using boken or jo, you learn to put yourself into the weapon, to extend beyond your physical body. You use it as an extension of your whole being. You put your mind into it and make yourself one with the weapon, and then you learn to project your mind and being through and beyond the weapon. Later, when you practice with a partner, you do the same. You become one with him/her, of the same mind. Finally, as you move through and complete the technique, your mind projects strongly and deliberately in order to properly lead and fully throw your partner.

On a practical side, always keep your weapons in good condition, checking for any cracks or splinters so as not to injure yourself or your partner. Avoid extended storage in car trunks, corners of rooms, or where temperature or humidity are extreme.

Use your weapons often so they don't lay around too long and begin to bow or bend. Using them is the best way to keep them in good shape, since the natural oils of your hands help to preserve them. Using wood oil is acceptable if you find your natural oils are too acidic and are reacting with the wood by breaking down the grain.

New weapons should be lightly sanded to remove any varnish applied for shipping and storage purposes. This will allow the grain to breathe and enhance the quality of your grip. In time, if the grain warrants it, you should sand the weapon again to keep it smooth and splinter free.

When using boken or jo be careful of walls, ceilings, lights, mirrors, priceless antique vases, fellow students, etc. Open your zanshin and be aware of these things both in front of and in back of you, as well as to your sides.

In all aspects of Aikido training, practice first for control, then for speed. Speed is empty without a firm foundation in the basics.

Never use someone else's weapons without his/her permission. When gathering your weapons after class, make absolutely sure you have your own and not someone else's. Like your gi, it is a good idea to mark your weapons for easy identification.

Some dojos stress weapon training heavily, while some reject it. Most believe in its value to some degree. The debate as to its necessity in "learning Aikido" will entertain practitioners for a long time to come. Different people may use different tools to reach the same end. The means may vary, but the result is the same.

If you follow the principles and adhere to the natural laws required in Aikido, you are on the right path.

Promotion and Advancement

"In your training, do not be in a hurry. Never think of yourself as an all-knowing, perfected master; you must continue to train daily with your friends and students and progress together in the Art of Peace."
                                                                                    —Morihei Ueshiba

A STUDENT WISHING TO test for rank must first accumulate the required minimum practice days. Once this is achieved, he/she should ask the chief instructor to evaluate his/her practice in order to determine if he/she is familiar enough with the required techniques. (Yamada Sensei's videos provide excellent detailed instruction and explanation of basic U.S.A.F. test requirements, listed on page 82.)

If permission is granted to prepare for testing, the student should begin concentrating on the required techniques for that rank. Students should be comfortable performing the techniques and performing the required ukemi when receiving them. In addition, it is good practice not only to be familiar with the requirements of the rank you wish to attain but those of the next rank as well. As you advance up the ranks you will still be responsible for knowing all of the previous rank's requirements.

If you need help in preparing for your test, ask your instructor or a senior student. They will be glad to help.

Private Lessons

Private lessons may be provided by the chief instructor in order to clarify specific problems. They are meant to supplement your regular class training, not replace it. Aikido is a group experience and one can never truly learn Aikido from the shelter and security of private lessons.

Testing

The purpose of testing is to give the student a passage by which to gauge his/her daily, monthly, and yearly practice. Tests are meant as an exhibition or demonstration of the student's level of understanding of Aikido principles and techniques.

Preparation for testing should begin well in advance of the actual test. Don't wait until the last minute and attempt to cram for it. If don't prepare properly, don't expect to pass or even be given permission to test.

Prior to testing you may be required to complete a minimum number of classes. You may also be required to submit a test application and pay a standard testing fee.

If you are considering testing for a rank, you should be very comfortable with the required techniques and the pace with which they should be performed. Your performance should demonstrate clearly that you have attained the proficiency required of that rank—and then some.

Testing is sometimes scheduled during or at the end of a seminar. When you are testing, it is strongly encouraged that you attend as much of that seminar as you can so your practice can be observed and evaluated. Be prepared to stay through the duration of all the tests. It is considered bad manners if you leave after your test is completed.

Even if you are not testing, you should support those who are by attending the testing. The best way to show that support is to be in your gi and sitting on the mat. If you are available for ukemi, bring it to the attention of your instructor.

While testing is in progress, all present should be respectful of the testing procedures. If you must talk, it should be done quietly. Keep movement to a minimum. Walking around, eating, drinking, or lounging is considered rude and distracting to the examiners, the participants, and to others in attendance.

Keep in mind that the point of Aikido training is not to focus exclusively on acquiring rank, but rather on bettering your character and relationship to your environment.

Conclusion

"When you reach real ability you will be able to become one with the enemy. Entering his heart you will see that he is not your enemy after all."

—Sword Master Tsuji (1650–1730)

WHETHER YOU TRAIN for one week or ten years, whether your goal is fifth kyu or shodan, make your true desire peace—both within you and around you. Then, whenever you find it, offer it to someone else.

In all things
choose peace,
because one moment you're here . . .

"The heaven and earth look so serene and beautiful. This Universe has revealed itself as a family created by the omnipresent God."
—Morihei Ueshiba

United States Aikido Federation Test Requirements

This list is included to give the reader an idea of basic testing requirements. However, requirements do vary from organization to organization and even from dojo to dojo.

5th Kyu (60 Days)
1. Shomenuchi Ikkyo (omote & ura)
2. Shomenuchi Iriminage
3. Katatetori Shihonage (omote & ura)
4. Ryotetori Tenchinage
5. Tsuki Kotegaeshi
6. Ushiro Tekubitori Kotegaeshi
7. Morotetori Kokyuho

4th Kyu (80 Days)
1. Shomenuchi Nikkyo (omote & ura)
2. Yokomenuchi Shihonage (omote & ura)
3. Tsuki Iriminage
4. Ushiro Tekubi Sankyo (omote & ura)
5. Ushiro Ryokatatori Kotegaeshi
6. Suwari Waza:
   Shomenuchi Ikkyo
   Katatori Nikkyo (omote & ura)
   Katatori Sankyo (omote & ura)

3rd Kyu (100 Days)
1. Yokomenuchi Iriminage (2 ways)

2. Yokomenuchi Kotegaeshi
3. Tsuki Kaitennage
4. Ushiro Ryokatatori Sankyo (omote & ura)
5. Morotetori Iriminage (2 ways)
6. Shomenuchi Sankyo (omote & ura)
7. Suwari Waza:
    Shomenuchi Iriminage
    Shomenuchi Nikkyo (omote & ura)
8. Hanmi Handachi: Katatetori Shihonage
    Katatetori Kaitennage
    (uchi & soto mawari*)

2nd Kyu (200 Days)
1. Shomenuchi Shihonage
2. Shomenuchi Kaitennage
3. Yokomenuchi Gokyo
4. Ushiro Tekubitori Shihonage
5. Ushiro Tekubitori Jujinage
6. Ushiro Kubishime Koshinage
7. Morotetori Nikkyo
8. Hanmi Handachi:
    Shomenuchi Iriminage
    Katatetori Nikkyo
    Yokomenuchi Kotegaeshi
9. Freestyle—2 persons

1st Kyu (300 Days)
1. Katatori Menuchi—5 techniques
2. Yokomenuchi—5 techniques
3. Morotetori—5 techniques

---

*Uchi and Soto Mawari—both inside (uchi) and outside (soto) movements.

4. Shomenuchi—5 techniques
5. Ryotetori—5 techniques
6. Koshinage—5 techniques
7. Tantotori
8. Hanmi Handachi (Ushiro Waza—5 techniques)
9. Freestyles—3 persons

Sho-Dan (400 Days)
1. All of 1st Kyu requirements
2. Tachitori
3. Jotori
4. Henkawaza**
5. Freestyle—4 persons

Ni-Dan (600 Days)
1. Attend 2 seminars per year after Sho-Dan
2. All of Sho-Dan requirements
3. Tachitori—2 persons
4. Freestyle—5 persons
5. Kaeshiwaza***

San-Dan (700 Days)
1. Attend two seminars per year after Ni-Dan. Subject of exam to be determined by examiner at the time of the exam.

Note: Day requirements are counted from the last test.

**Henkawaza—switching from one technique to another. Examiner will call the first technique.
***Kaeshiwaza—counter techniques. Uke applies the technique to nage. Original techniques will be called by examiner (e.g. to apply sankyo against nikkyo).

Glossary of Words of Attack

1. Hanmi Handachi—uke standing, nage sitting
2. Jotori—jo disarming
3. Katatetori—one hand grab to wrist
4. Katatori—one hand grab to the shoulder
5. Morotetori—two hands on one
6. Ryotetori—both wrists grabbed from the front
7. Shomenuchi—strike to forehead
8. Yokomenuchi—Strike to the side of the head
9. Suwariwaza—technique from sitting
10. Tachitori—boken disarming
11. Tantotori—knife disarming
12. Tsuki—Thrust or punch
13. Ushiro Kubishime—choke from behind with free hand grabbing wrist
14. Ushiro Ryokatatori—both shoulders grabbed from behind
15. Ushiro Tekubitori—both wrists grabbed from behind
16. Ushiro Waza—any attack from behind

Aikido reference videos

by Yoshimitsu Yamada 8th Dan, Chairman U.S.A.F.

The Power and the Basics 1—Aikido basics and 5th Kyu requirements.

The Power and the Basics 2—Additional Aikido basics, 4th and 3rd Kyu requirements.

Contact:
Susan Wolk
U.S.A.F. Eastern Region
98 State Street
Northampton, MA 01060

Aikido Terms

This is a sampling of terminology common to many Aikido dojos. some dojos may use other terms in addition to those listed below.

Ai (Eye)
Harmony, coming together, love.

Aikido (Eye-key-doe)
Ai = harmony, Ki = spirit, Do = The way or path.

Aiki-ken (Eye-key-ken)
Swordsmanship. According to the principles of Aikido.

Aiki Taiso (Eye-key-tie-so)
Aikido exercises.

Ai Hanmi (Eye-hon-me)
Equal stance.

Ai Uchi (Eye-ooh-chee)
Equal strike or equal kill.

Atemi (Ah-tem-ee)
Defensive strike to distract or unbalance your partner so a technique can be effectively applied. It is not meant to inflict injury.

Boken (Bow-ken)
Wooden sword used in practice.

Budo (Boo-doe)
Bujutso techniques of war.

Bushido (Boo-she-doe)
Warrior's Code—The way of the warrior.

Chudan (Chew-don)
Middle position.

Dan (Don)
Aikido grade holder, black belt rank.

Dojo (Doe-joe)
Training hall (formerly a term used by Buddhist priests in reference to their place of worship).

Dori (Door-ree)
Grab.

Dosa (Doh-sah)
An exercise.

Doshi (Doe-she)
Comrade, friend (used among fellow Aikidoists).

Iie (Ee-ay)
No.

Fukushidoin (Foo-koo-she-doe-in)
First instructors rank (2nd or 3rd Dan).

Gaeshi (Guy-eh-she)
To reverse.

Gedan (Gay-don)
Low position.

Gi (Ghee)
Training uniform.

Gyaku Hanmi (Ghee-ah-koo hon-me)
Opposite stance.

Gyaku Te-dori (Ghee-ah-koo tay-doe-ree)
Cross hand grab (right to right or left to left).

Hai (Hi)
Yes.

Hakama (Hah-kah-mah)
A divided, pant-like skirt.

Hanmi (Hon-me)
A posture in which one foot is advanced one step and the body weight is distributed equally on both feet. Triangular stance.

Hanmi Handachi (Hon-me Hon-dah-chee)
Nage (thrower) is kneeling and opponent (the attacker), approaches from a standing position.

Hantai (Hahn-tie)
Opposite or reverse.

Hara (Har-ah)
The center of existence. Lower abdomen, physical and spiritual center.

Hidari (He-dah-ree)
Left (direction).

Hiji (He-jee)
Elbow.

Hiji-dori (He-jee-doe-ree)
Elbow grab.

Iaido (Ee-eye-do)
The art of drawing the sword.

Iaito (Ee-eye-toe)
Practice sword for Iaido.

Itai (Ee-tie)
"It hurts."

Irimi (Ee-ree-me)
To enter; entering.

Jinja (Jin-jah)
Shrine.

Jodan (Joe-don)
High position.

Jyu (Gee-you)
Free style.

Jyu Waza (Gee-you Wah-zah)
Free style techniques/practice.

Jo (Joe)
Wooden staff.

Kaiten (Kai-ten)
To revolve or rotate.

Kaiten-nage (Kai-ten-nah-gay)
Rotary throw.

Kami (Kah-mee)
Very simply stated: spirits; gods.

Kata (Kah-tah)
Shoulder. Also means "form" practice of pre-arranged exercise(s).

Kata-dori (Kah-tah-doe-ree)
Shoulder grab.

Katate (Kah-tah-tay)
One hand (left or right).

Katana (Kah-tah-nah)
Long sword.

Keiko (Kay-ko)
Practice session; training.

Ken (Ken)
Japanese sword.

Ki (Key)
Spirit. The vital force of the body; Universal Energy; a stream or flow of positive energy.

Kihon (Key-hohn)
Basic form of a technique.

Ki-no-nagare (Key-noh-nah-gah-ree)
Fluid form of a technique.

Ki Musubi (Key-Moo-su-bee)
Ki blending.

Kiai (Key-eye)
A piercing scream or cry with practical and psychological value, meaning "Meeting of the spirits."

Kokyu (Coke-you)
Breath power . . . the coordination of ki flow with breathing.

Kokyu Dosa (Coke-you Doe-sah)
A method of off-balancing and pinning your partner with your "ki" instead of your physical power.

Kohai (Koh-hi)
Junior or subordinate student.

Koshi (Koh-she)
Hips, waist (also spelled Goshi).

Koshi-nage (Koh-she-nah-gay)
Hip throw.

Kote-gaeshi (Koh-teh-guy-eh-she)
Wrist turn out throw.

Kumi-jo (Koo-mee-joe)
Advanced partner practices with jo.

Kumi-tachi (Koo-mee-tah-chee)
Advanced partner practices with ken.

Kyu (Cue or Kee-you)
Aikido rank, class. A *mudansha,* or undergraduate.

Ma-ai (Mah-eye)
Distance between uke and nage, meaning "harmony of space."

Men (Men)
Face, head.

Men-uchi (Men-oo-chee)
Strike to the head.

Mig (Mee-gee)
Right (direction).

Misogi (Miss-o-gee)
Purification.

Mitsuke (Mits-skay)
Eye focusing and direction.

Mokuso (Mock-so)
Meditate.

Morote-dori (Moh-roh-tay-doe-ree)
Attack holding one wrist/forearm with both hands.

Musubi (Moo-soo-bee)
Blending.

Nage (Nah-gay)
Throw. The person who throws.

Obi (Oh-bee)
Belt.

Omote (Oh-moe-tay)
Moving in front (forward).

Omote Sankaku (Oh-moe-tay-sahn-kah-koo)
Forward triangular stance.

O Sensei (Oh-sen-say)
The great teacher (Morehei Ueshiba).

Oyo-waza (Oh-yoh wah-zah)
Variations on basic technique.

Randori (Ran-door-ri)
Multiple attack.

Rei (Ray)
Salutation, bow.

Reigi (Ray-ghee)
Etiquette.

Ryote (Ree-oh-tay)
Both hands.

Ryote-dori (Ree-oh-tay-doe-ree)
Both hands grabbed by both hands.

Samurai (Sam-oh-rye)
Military retainer (feudal period).

Sempai (Sem-pie)
Senior student.

Sensei (Sen-say)
Teacher, instructor.

Seiza (Say-zah)
Formal sitting posture.

Shidoin (She-doe-in)
Certified Instructor rank (4th or 5th Dan).

Shihan (She-han)
Master Instructor (6th Dan and above) — A title reserved for the highest ranking teachers.

Shiho (She-ho)
Four directions.

Shiho-nage (She-ho-nah-gay)
Four directions throw.

Shodan (Show-don)
Holder of the first grade black belt.

Shomen (Show-men)
Front or top of the head.

Shomen-uchi (Show-men-oo-chee)
Strike to the top front of the head.

Shugyo (Shoo-g-yo)
Rigorous daily training for overall purification.

Suburi (Sue-boo-ree)
A single movement using the ken or jo, done as a solo practice.

Suwari Waza or *Shikko* (Sue-wah-ree Wah-zah) or (She-ko)
Sitting techniques.

Tachi (Tah-Chee)
Japanese sword.

Tachi-Dori (Tah-chee Door-ree)
Sword disarming.

Taijutsu (Tie-jut-sue)
Body arts. The techniques of Aikido done without weapons.

Tai No Henko (Tie-no-hen-ko)
The basic blending practice. Tenkan exercise.

Tai Sabaki (Tie-sa-bocki)
Body movements.

Tanden (Tahn-den)
Point just below the navel. "One point." "Hara."

Tanto (Tahn-toe)
Wooden knife.

Te (Tay)
Hand.

Tegatana (Tay-gah-tah-nah)
Hand blade. Sword edge of the hand.

Te Kubi (Tay-koo-be)
Wrist.

Tenchi (Ten-shee)
Ten = heaven, Chi = earth. A position of the hands, one high (up) and one low (down).

Tenchi-nage (Ten-shee-nah-gay)
Heaven and earth throw.

Tenkan (Ten-kahn)
To turn.

Tsuki (T'ski)
Thrust.

Uchi (Oo-chee)
To strike.

Uke (Oo-kay)
The person who gives the attack and receives the technique. Generally speaking, "uke" refers to the person being thrown.

Ukemi (Oo-kem-me)
The art of receiving the technique and falling away from harm. Includes rolling and break falls (high falls).

Ura (Oo-rah)
Moving behind.

Ura Sankaku (Oo-rah-sahn-kah-koo)
Reverse triangular stance.

Ushiro (Oo-she-row)
Back, behind, rear.

Ushiro Eri-dori (Oo-she-row Ear-ree doe-ree)
Collar grab from behind.

Ushiro Hiji-dori (Oo-she-row Hee-jee-doe-ree)
Elbows grabbed from the rear.

Ushiro Ryo-kata-dori (Oo-she-row Ree-oh-kah-tah-doe-ree)
Both shoulders grabbed from behind.

Ushiro Ryote-dori (Oo-she-row Ree-oh-tay-doe-ree)
Both wrists grabbed from behind.

Ushiro Kubi-shime (Oo-she-row Koo-bee-she-may)
Choking with one hand around the neck from the rear, usually while holding one wrist with the free hand.

Ushiro-dori (Oo-she-row-doe-ree)
Bear hug from behind.

Waza (Wah-zah)
Techniques.

Yokomen (Yoh-ko-men)
Side of the head.

Yokomen-uchi (Yoh-ko-men-oo-chee)
Strike to the side of the head.

Yudansha (You-don-sha)
Black belt grade holder(s).

Zanshin (Zahn-shin)
Unbroken awareness and concentration.

Zazen (Zah-zen)
Sitting meditation.

Phrases

Ohayo / Ohayo gozaimasu (Ohio go-zah-ee-mahs)
Good morning (used before 10:00 AM).

Konnichi wa (Kone-knee-chee-wa)
Hello! Good day (after 10:00 AM).

Komban wa (Comb-bahn wah)
Good evening.

Oyasumi nasai (Oh-yah-sue-me nah-sigh)
Good night (before bedtime).

Sayonara (Sigh-yoh-nah-rah)
Good-bye.

Domo / Domo Arigato
(Doe-moe / Doe-moe-ah-ree-gah-toe)
Thank you.

Arigato Gozaimasu
(Ah-ree-gah-toe go-zah-ee-mahss)
Thank you (very polite).

Sensei, domo arigato Gozaimashita
(Sen-say, doe-moe ah-ree-gah-toe go-zah-ee-mah-she-tah)
Thank you very much for what you have done (spoken by
students at the end of Aikido class).

Onegai Shimasu (Oh-nigh-guy-she-mahss)
I make a request (spoken when one wishes to practice with
a fellow student or teacher).

Gomen Nasai (Go-men nah-sigh)
I'm sorry, excuse me.

Do itashimashite (Doe ee-tah-she-mah-she-tay)
Don't mention it. You're welcome.

Ogen'ki Desu ka (Oh-ghen-key des-kah)
How are you? Are you in good spirits?

Okagesama de (Ohkah-ghe-sama day)
Fine, thank you.

Hajime (Hah-jee-may)
Begin.

Mate (Mah-tay)
Wait.

Yame (Yah-may)
Stop.

Itchi (Itch)
One.

Ni (Nee)
Two.

San (Sahn)
Three.

Shi (She)
Four.

Go (Goh)
Five.

Roku (Roke)
Six.

Shichi (Shich-ee)
Seven.

Hachi (Hach)
Eight.

Ku (Koo)
Nine.

Ju (Joo)
Ten.

Ikkyo (Ee-kio)
First technique.

Nikkyo (Nee-kio)
Second technique.

Sankyo (Son-kio)
Third technique.

Yonkyo (Yon-kio)
Fourth technique.

Gokyo (Go-kio)
Fifth technique.

Suggested Reading

Chitwood, Dr. T. *How To Defend Yourself Without Even Trying.* Sioux Falls, SD: Polstar International, 1981. Philosophy.

Crane, R. & K. *Aikido In Training.* Berlin, NJ: Cool Rain, 1993. Technique, history, philosophy.

Crum, Thomas F. *The Magic Of Conflict.* New York, NY: Simon & Schuster, 1987. Aikido principles for conflict resolution.

Dobson, Terry. *Aikido In Everyday Life.* Berkeley, CA: North Atlantic Books, 1992. Aikido principles for daily living and conflict resolution.

Heckler, Richard. *Aikido and The New Warrior.* Berkeley, CA: North Atlantic Books, 1985. Various articles by Aikidoists.

Homma, Gaku. *Aikido For Life.* Berkeley, CA: North Atlantic Books, 1990. Mat and living advice.

Kamata, S., and K. Shimizo. *Zen and Aikido.* Tokyo, Japan: Aiki News, 1992. Comparisons of Zen and Aikido.

Klickstein, Bruce. *Living Aikido.* Berkeley, CA: North Atlantic Books, 1987. Technique and training advice.

Pranin, Stan. *Aikido Masters.* Tokyo, Japan: Aiki News, 1992. Pre-war students of O Sensei.

Pranin, Stan. *Aiki News Encyclopedia Of Aikido.* Tokyo, Japan: Aiki News, 1991. General information.

Saito, Morihiro. *Aikido—Its Heart and Appearance.* Tokyo, Japan: Minato, 1975. Basic techniques.

Saito, Morihiro. *Traditional Aikido, Vol. 1–5.* Tokyo, Japan: Minato, 1973. Technique.

Saotome, Mitsugi. *Aikido And The Harmony Of Nature.* Boulogne, France: Sedirep, 1985. Philosophy, history.

Saotome, Mitsugi. *The Principles Of Aikido.* Boston, MA: Shambhala, 1989. Philosophy, technique.

Shioda, Gozo. *Dynamic Aikido.* New York, NY: Kodansha, 1968. Technique.

Stevens, John. *Abundant Peace.* Boston, MA: Shambhala, 1987. A biography of the Morihei Ueshiba.

Stevens, J. and K. Shirata. *Aikido—The Way Of Harmony.* Boston, MA: Shambhala, 1984. Technique, history.

Tohei, Koichi. *Aikido In Daily Life.* Tokyo, Japan: Rikugei, 1966. Philosophy.

Ueshiba, Kisshomaru. *Aikido.* Tokyo, Japan: Kodansha, 1974. Technique, history, philosophy.

Ueshiba, Kisshomaru. *The Spirit Of Aikido.* Tokyo, Japan: Kodansha, 1984. Philosophy, history.

Ueshiba, Morihei. *The Art Of Peace.* Boston, MA: Shambhala 1992. Words of the Founder of Aikido.

Ueshiba, Morihei. *Budo.* New York, NY: Kodansha, 1991. History, technique.

Westbrook , A. and O. Ratti. *Aikido And The Dynamic Sphere.* Rutland, VT: Charles E. Tuttle, 1970. Philosophy, technique, history.

Yamada, Y. and S. Pimsler. *The New Aikido Complete.* New York, NY: Lyle Stuart, 1981. Technique.

Publications:

Aikido Today Magazine
Susan Perry, Editor
1420 North Claremont Boulevard, #111B
Claremont, CA 91711 USA

Aiki News
Stan Pranin, Editor
Tamagawa Gakuen
5-11-25-204, Machida-shi,
Tokyo-to 194 Japan

About the Author

Greg O'Connor is co-founder of Aikido Schools of New Jersey, and the chief instructor of ASNJ's Morristown and Clifton dojos. He began his training in traditional Japanese martial arts in 1972 with Japanese/Okinawan karate. In 1976, he made a commitment to the study of Aikido. Since then he has traveled extensively in Japan and elsewhere to study with the world's top Aikido masters. He is one of the few full-time professional Aikido teachers in the United States and currently holds the rank of 4th Dan, Shidoin, with the United States Aikido Federation Eastern Region under Shihan Yoshimitsu Yamada, 8th Dan.

In addition to teaching and continuing his Aikido training, Greg actively supports and pursues ways of introducing Aikido's principles and alternatives to people who may never find themselves on an Aikido dojo mat.

Along with Aikido, Greg studies and teaches Iaido (the way of the sword), and also practices the arts of Kyudo (Japanese archery) and Ikebana (Japanese flower arrangement). He is an experienced graphic designer, artist, cartoonist, mountain climber and backpacker, and a certified massage therapist.

One of the many gifts Aikido has given him is his wife, Mary Kay, whom he met on an East Coast Summer Camp mat.

Please feel free to send comments or suggestions to:

Greg O'Connor
Aikido Schools of New Jersey
42 Bank Street
Morristown, NJ 07960

AIKIDO SCHOOLS
OF NEW JERSEY

Photo Acknowledgments:

pg. 3   Mitsogi Saotome
pg. 11   Jeff Chilton
pg. 12   Yoshimitsu Yamada /Gary Samuels
pg. 14   Mitsogi Saotome
pg. 81   Kazuo Chiba
pg. 105 Jeff Altschul